GW01071947

Two Stories

JEANETTE WINTERSON

HAY FESTIVAL PRESS

2005

Published by
Hay Festival Press
The Drill Hall, 25 Lion Street
Hay HR3 5AD, United Kingdom

www.hayfestival.com

Copyright © Jeanette Winterson 2005

ISBN 0 9547168 3 3

1,000 copies (of which 100 have been
numbered and signed by the author)
have been printed on Simili Japon paper
and casebound by MPG BOOKS LTD,
Bodmin, Cornwall

Designed and typeset in Ehrhardt
by Five Seasons Press, Hereford

CONTENTS

The Night Sea Voyage

CREAKING IS WHAT I REMEMBER. Creak of boards (the ship), creak of joints (mine), the wooden parrot cage swinging over the Captain's table. The cello expanding in its case. The biscuit barrels wind-dried. The soaked oak water barrels, coopered hoops rust-blistered.

A cockroach-creaking, rat-rattling, cage-clattering, tub-thumping, head-banging, wrist-slitting, noose from nowhere, neck-breaking sea voyage of suicides, misfits, vermin, stowaways, rentboys, alkies, sniffers, poppers, mainliners, punks, sailors, dolls, and me.

Business on board? To avoid the Hand of Fate. And all the rest of Fate's Body Parts too. I want a quiet life—no fifteen minutes of fame, no news headlines, no minor memorial, no speeches, no widow, no example to the faint-hearted. I *am* the faint-hearted. Somebody has to be weak, cowardly, ill-equipped, unprepared. I am the one who burns the toast, misses the bus, never has a candle in a power cut. Those are small failures I know, but even my inadequacies are inadequate. The Titanic had too few lifeboats; that was a disaster. I don't have enough buttons on my shirt; that's me.

My name is Jonah.

I don't know if any of you reading this deposit has ever run away to sea. In the old days, a fresh start was as simple as the next clipper out of Deptford. Sunk in debt? Raise the anchor. Wife? Scuttle her. Too many children, bed-packed like sardines? Go fishing. Wanted by the police? Swim for it. The best antidote to a beached life was to get afloat. I thought I could do that, but I ended belly up. Very big belly up. Whale size.

The other Jonah, the one who sits inside me as I sit inside this whale was also the swallowed kind. If you recall, God told him to go to Ninevah to warn the inhabitants to repent of their sins before it was TOO LATE. Instead, Jonah jumped on a ship to Tarshish, forgetting that God made the sea as well as the land, and that he was the first person to own night-vision equipment. We know this from reading the very beginning of the Bible (AKA the word of God) where God says 'Let there be light'. Only a guy who could see in the dark would make such a statement on behalf of the rest of us. Fruitless then, a true-life *yes we have no bananas* situation, to try and get a ship at bedtime, and make a dash for it. HE was bound to notice. HE did.

In preferred retribution mode, God sent a powerful storm (cf. The Flood, Genesis 6) to rock the boat.

When the boat was well and truly rocked, the Captain realised that someone on board must be responsible (this was before the days of coincidence), and Jonah had to confess. Pragmatic, but without mercy, the Captain threw Jonah overboard to save his ship.

The winds dropped immediately, because God was watching, and the last thing the Captain saw was a huge rock rise out of the waters (God likes to call his water 'waters'), and then the rock opened its mouth and swallowed Jonah, thus saving him from drowning, but causing severe distress long before anyone in the world carried Rescue Remedy.

Jonah was in the belly of the whale.

Let me tell you a thing or two about whales. *The arteries of a whale are so wide a child could crawl through them.*

It was a tumbling, rumbling, legs and arms slide down the thick throat and into the stinking chamber of the whale. Jonah landed on a mattress of fat and sank up to his armpits in seal blubber. The whale belly was a chemical cauldron of fish-blistering enzymes. In front of Jonah's nose, and he wished he didn't have one, was a whole shark, eight feet long, slowly turning in its fermenting bath, like a piece of modern art.

The whale was not a fussy eater. This belly was a ruinous rotting mass of fish guts, nets, boat tackle and plankton. Jonah could see all this because God let him see it. It was not pitch black, but dimly lit and greeny-grey. It wasn't hell, but it was a near relative.

Jonah had no family. No one would miss him.

Jonah sighed, and his breath rippled the blubber cushioning his chin. He could die here, or he could die over there, where a rusty anchor was propped in the corner of the belly of the whale. It was not much of a choice, but making it was a way of staying alive, so he squirmed his way out of the clotting cold mess, and went, blubber-hung, to scrape himself clean on the iron anchor.

The whale swam on through the Deep (see Waters).

So what of me?

I sailed so fast out of my life that the land had disappeared before I had time to set a course for anywhere else. Friends cheered me on, waved from the dockside, then went home to watch TV, and after the first flush of self-congratulation and a bottle of rum, I realised I had no idea where I was heading or how to get there.

Then night came and I was alone.

A week later, it was still night.

The sun did not rise. The light did not begin to dissolve the sea-shadows. It was a starless moonless night. It was black like on the inside of something bigger than you are.

A night-box. A black hole, padded cell of darkness.

This was supposed to be an escape not a prison.

It was supposed to be a modest escape too. I am not built for the hero's life, and when the hero-hour came ticking by my door, I decided to run for it. Why would anyone want to do God's bidding if they could do something else instead?

I have to tell you that I don't believe in God, but I do believe in something like private revelation, and I know that on the day I went to sea, the day had come to stop being a small-minded, hand-wringing, hang-dog, head-down, no-eye-contact type, and LIVE what was left of my life. I put that

17

in Capitals, partly for emphasis and partly because it is what unhinged people do, put things in Capitals, and as far as hinges go, my door out onto the world was nailed shut long ago. I have no hinges. I let nothing out and I let nothing in. I live a boarded-up life with just a spy-hole to look suspiciously out on intruders.

From behind my defences I can say that nothing has really touched me, mattered to me, or made a difference to me. Then, I woke up one day, to find the Hand of Fate, or something very like it, pointing at ME, in the shape of LOVE. Love, love, love, and not even a girl or a boy, but a searing sense of a world as big as I was little, as extravagant as I was plain, as maddening as I was timid, a risky, lurching, juggling high-wire world, wearing coloured clothes carelessly, sometimes going naked, a world as improbable as I was predictable, a world as weird as I was dull.

I woke up, yes just like that, and the world was weird. The known, safe, media-managed world had shrunk to a scripted joke, and the strange, scary untamed world of terror and glory was expanding outside the axe-smashed panel of my nailed-up door.

Life had got tired of waiting and come for me.

'Someone else,' I bleated, 'someone else, because this world is too dazzling if it is true. I cannot bear it. Take it away. Give me back the grey-greeny world where it's not my fault and there's nothing I can do.'

Let there be light? 40w bulb on a timer, please.

And then I discovered that if you run away from the Moment—(just a Capital letter this time, please note, so maybe things are improving a bit), anyway, if you run away from the Moment (and only you know what the Moment is), then the night sea voyage begins. They don't tell you how complete is the darkness, or how long, or how hopeless. They give you pills, tell you to move on, tell you to have therapy with some re-trained out-of-work actor, but they don't say that this night will fit you close as a skin, a dark twin who knows your soul. They don't say 'soul', but soul it is. Your soul grafted in darkness.

My funny little grey world of mostly rain and weak sun is gone. It is night now, true night, and the sea is everywhere. I will just have to wait.

I find I have no paradigm for waiting.

Waiting is what happens on budget flights and the night before the Sales start, and the day before bad news. Alpha males and celebrities never wait, and people who do wait are lower down the food chain—which brings me back to Jonah, boiled down to a fish-bite in the belly of the whale.

For three days and three nights he waited. Stench, sweat, bile, fermentation, gas, rot, fumes, and worst of all, new occupants, swordfish, octopus, fins, suckers, marble eyes, seaweed, a goat, the goat alive like him, and living inside the fatty vaulted acid-attacked cell.

He longed for Ninevah. If only he had gone to the City of Sin. He sat with his head in his hands, his heart in his boots, and his boots in blubber. The goat sat with him, looking at him with its square double pupils, its udders all milky with memories of land.

As for me, I learned to crawl along the arteries of my affliction.

I am crawling like one of those children who pulled coal wagons in the depths of the earth. I am on my hands and knees listening to the boom boom above, or is it my pulse, my heart? I don't know. I must pull this weight strapped behind me, this cart filled with my own fears and inadequacies, and if there is a way out, perhaps I will find it, but not until my hands and knees have worn away the sadness in me, sadness so deep that a whale could swim in its waters and never be found.

I do not know anymore what is inside and what is outside. Am I inside the whale or is the whale inside me?

He is the largest mammal on the planet. He is a mammal and not a fish. He is a mammal like me. He *is* me, this whale.

Wait.

Slowly I stopped thinking of bus-stops and supermarket check-outs, and I began to think of spring waiting until winter has done its work, its dark, underground work.

I began to think of the child in the womb.

I began to think of love and its patience. I began to think of the universe before it was able to exist. I began to think of continental shifts and tectonic plates, of centuries of ice, and molten suns. I began to think of human beings evolving out of clubs and animal skins. I thought of the time it takes to know anything at all—really know it, and the time it takes for one thing gradually to become another.

And yet, the moment when it happens bears no trace of the waiting. The bulbs flower, the child is born, the universe bursts into stars and this small blue planet becomes a world. Somewhere in time, a creature stands upright. Somewhere in time, so will I stand upright.

People marvel—they say they saw no sign of the happening before it happened. No. It was done in darkness. This is the night sea voyage.

On the third day Jonah noticed a thin light penetrating his prison. It was not the grey-greeny light he had learned to see by, it was less muddy, less foul. It was clean light, he thought, and then, he felt the floor rising, and he realised that the whale was breaking the waves. The whale was in the light, and so too was Jonah.

There was a belching and a retching and a grating like the gates of Hell opening, and a wind that sucked him out like the wind at the end of time when the world will disappear again into the tiny place it hid before time. He was being drawn up through the cavity of the whale, and as he flew, this proto-astronaut, weightless, propelled, he had the sense to grab the goat by the rope, and the two of them sailed through the gasping vomiting throat and straight out onto the beach, bam!

Yes, BAM! Blubber-bound, becalmed, and beginning again. They looked up out of eyes filmed with sludge, and there was the pier, and the Grand Hotel, and all the sinners going up and down as intolerant and self-righteous as ever, and Jonah thought, 'I will tell them to repent and to be kind to the shipwrecked and the goats, and to give up their wicked ways, and stop persecuting others and waging war where there is none, and I will tell them all this even if they don't listen, and what I will tell them most of all is not to TURN AWAY.

He shouted that out.

I heard him. His shout skimmed across the waves like a smooth flat stone, bouncing the white tops and hitting my ship so that the ship began to sink. The water was pouring in, the ship was going down. It was a splitting, shuddering, rivet-popping, board-breaking, collapsing, sinking, planked-up wreck of a journey. It was the end.

I don't know what saved me, but there was a light-belt and I wriggled into it, until the sea threw me onto a stretch of coast I had never seen before. What did I expect? That the voyage would take me home. The prow of the ship nosing into my living room at dawn?

The night sea voyage will deliver you to the place you never wanted to be—the place you saw on the map and said 'NO!'

Here it is—Ilyria, Bohemia, or some other shore, fierce, unknown, savage, new-found. But the sun is rising in red reflection on the sea. The voyage is done. The journey begins.

The White Room

THE WHITE ROOM IS NOT MINE. One window frames an ash tree. One window lenses the world.

From the wide lens of your window I can see an album of ordinary life. There's a woman unfolding a music stand with metallic determination. She picks up a flute, begins to play, and soap bubbles of notes break against your glass. The music is floating but the woman is standing very still. The strange thing about her is that she is naked. Yes, quite naked, her spine as long and straight as her flute, her vertebrae like the keys of the flute.

I pushed up the window to let in the music. We were floating Mozart. Why is it that the real things are fragile and tough, destroyed so easily, but never damaged? Lost to us endlessly—stupidly, unknowingly—but in themselves always found again, when time opens like a door.

And the stories are full of people trying to find a door they swear they found once before; the green door in the green hill. The door that leads nowhere, the door that leads to the only place you can go. The door marked destiny that is really desire. The dream door, the death door, the door that separates your past, and now, forever.

34

The stories advise me that one day the hill will open, in the shining hour, when time and space and desire *hinge* the solid world into a door.

The white room is a chapel.

Like all sacred spaces, it does and does not exist. It has joists and floorboards and damp and doorjambs. It can be bought and sold. At the same time, what is valuable here cannot be traded in the market-place. What is valuable here is a quality of light. Light that changes as we do. Light as subtle and uncatchable as human beings.

We are fallen angels netted in light.

The white room is a hospital.

It happens on the borders between healing and pain. The light is as surgical as a laser. The light finds me out. My soft tissue is exposed. Parts of me have been cut away.

I had a wound that would not heal. You rummaged your hands through it and it bled again. It bled clean this time, and the poison left me. That wound has been infected for years. It will never heal but it is not infected anymore.

My body is clean.

The white room is a mystery.

The owner is often away. Time sleeps here—among the sixteenth-century furniture and the twenty-first-century life.

Some people buy antiques because they are old—other people buy them because they are still alive.

Time can be caught in objects.

When I touch this table where a woman counted out her past like money, I too start to bargain with life—what will this cost me? What can I expect in return?

She tells me the old story, her fingers stroking her memories. Time is tarnished, but not where she touches it—where she touches it, time is worn thin from being turned over. Time thin enough to lose between floorboards. Time worn bright with love.

Love is the story. This story. This time.

The white room is where we made love.

We had met a week before in a restaurant
and I knew something was changing when
I was envious of the salt cellar. You were
playing with the neck of the salt cellar while
we talked. My neck tingled.

I notice people's hands. They say more
than the obvious body parts.

I don't know how to read your palm, but
I can read the sex in your hands. You will be
a good lover. I shouldn't be thinking about
that, but I am.

We talked. I have no memory of our
conversation. I remember everything about
that day, but nothing of what was said. We
used words as a screen to hide our thoughts.
The screen was black and white and made of
bamboo and rice paper. Behind the screen I

was dreaming in colour and the thin screen was punched through.

'Do you like Japanese food?' 'Yes,' I said, 'yes.' 'Do you go to the theatre?' 'Yes,' I said, 'yes.' 'Should we go and see a film?' And I'm thinking *should we go and see? Should we go? Should we . . . ?*

Wondering if we should I knew we would, with an inevitability that felt like fate, which is dangerous, because life is not fate, life is choice. It is easier if things happen to us, but truer that we happen to things. I had wanted this moment so much I had birthed it, fleshed it, fucked it, before it happened. I knew it would happen. The only things I couldn't know were *when* and *who*.

It is today. It is you. The door is opening.

You are not the door, but you are the burst of light that has thrown the rest of time into shadow. I will go through the light because this is what I said I wanted, a runic longing I was reluctant to read. I write the plain text of my heart in a script I cannot read. Writing but not reading—like most of us I suppose, for whom control is the act of doing, and loss is the recognition of what we have done.

What is desire?

Desire is a restaurant. Desire is watching you eat. Desire is pouring wine for you. Desire is looking at the menu and wondering what it would be like to kiss you. Desire is the surprise of your skin.

Look—in between us now are the props of ordinary life—glasses, knives, cloths. Time has been here before us. History has had you—and me too. My hand has brushed against yours for centuries. The props change, but not this. Not this single naked wanting you.

Slightest accidents open up new worlds.

It had been raining and someone had taken my umbrella. I had to shelter under yours, bodies close together, respectably close. Drops of rain fell from the down-turned nylon edges of our stripy canopy. Each was a complete world, new and untried, a crystal ball that held the future we would choose. Let them fall. There are so many chances, so many worlds, pouring down on us. Like most people I take no notice and let them flow away, aeons breaking back into the universes where they were made. We are universes dripping with worlds. All we have to do is choose.

I have no choice, is what I usually say. Not true.

We were wet through before we got back to your room. You dried my hair in a towel. I put your shoes on the radiator. Simple gestures that take on meaning, and I wondered why it is only in these heightened moments that the significance of everything is clear. Is it too much to live with so much meaning? I don't watch the signs to see if they are auspicious, and I am not superstitious, but all of us could be clairvoyant if we were not so afraid of what we might see. I don't mean doom and disaster, I hardly mean anything sizeable at all, only the living texture of each moment and each gesture. The feel of life under my fingers, sometimes rough, sometimes impossibly fine, and I could read it like Braille, but I don't because I daren't.

Into the clockwork universe comes the quantum child. Potential, dimension, multiplicity, miracle. Teach him to tell the time as fast as you can or he might not know there is only one life, and he might risk everything to find another.

I know that the universe is unpredictable and wild, and that every birth is cosmos-hurled. I know that none of us can live like that, and we say with pride that *everything is going like clockwork.* The cliché protects and reveals as clichés do. Eventually, in every life, the clock will stop to let in time—the impossible longed-for moment, where life is rolled up like a ball and flung back at us. It is a moment of choice, a moment where past present and future are constellated. In the constellation of our bodies we discover a new star. How shall we name it? How shall we follow it? And if we follow it, to what unlikely beginning will it lead?

I will cross continents of history and geographies of time. I will be the place where the story starts.

A woodcutter had three sons. The first was so strong that he could chop down an oak tree in a morning. The second was so skilled that he could plank up the wood in an afternoon. The third son was so small that he just collected the acorns.

'And what is the use of that?' said his father

'You never know when you might need a forest,' replied the son.

What happens next has no practical purpose. What happens next belongs in the forest of my dreams. What happens next is not sensible or industrious. I have arrived at the borders of commonsense and either I

Jeanette Winterson

turn back to my own land, or I cross into a place where different laws prevail.

The rain has fallen all night and I am out of my depth. What did you say? *My body is a river deep enough for diving—swim in me.*

What happens if I don't turn back? What happens if I choose the river?

My heart is beating. The second that beats between your life and mine. I am leaning over the water, but it's not my own reflection that I see, the water is too troubled for that. What I can see is the world turned upside down, a watery city, the mirror of the solid world that I have now. But everything solid is turning into its watery equivalent. There is nothing to hold on to, I shall have to let go.

There is something to hold on to. You have put out your hand. For the first time I touch your skin, skin close enough for grafting. Graft this moment on to time and take it with us when the clock starts ticking again, which will happen very soon. Time stops rarely and not for long. The door opens but no one can say when.

Make love to me.

This is the door that finally swings free. The door at the top of the stairs in your recurring dream. This is the forbidden door that can only be opened with a bloodstained key. This is the door that sets the prisoner free. This is the door at the edge of the world. This is the door that opens on to a river fished with stars.

Open me. Pass through me, and whatever lies on the other side could not be reached except by this. This you. This now. This caught moment opening into a lifetime.

There is music in the room. This room is ours.

Other titles in the
Hay Festival Press
uniform series
(*available from* www.hayfestival.com)

BOTTLE
Margaret Atwood
2004

A NIGHT OFF FOR PRUDENTE DE MORAES
Louis de Bernières
2004

MEETING CÉZANNE
Michael Morpurgo
2005